NTSB/RAR-08/01
PB2008-916301
Notation 7992A
Adopted March 18, 2008

I0428089

Railroad Accident Report

Collision of Massachusetts Bay Transportation Authority Train 322
and Track Maintenance Equipment Near
Woburn, Massachusetts
January 9, 2007

**National
Transportation
Safety Board**

490 L'Enfant Plaza, S.W.
Washington, D.C. 20594

National Transportation Safety Board. 2008. *Collision of Massachusetts Bay Transportation Authority Train 322 and Track Maintenance Equipment near Woburn, Massachusetts, January 9, 2007.* **Railroad Accident Report NTSB/RAR-08/01. Washington, DC.**

Abstract: On Tuesday, January 9, 2007, at 1:38 p.m., southbound Massachusetts Bay Transportation Authority passenger train 322 operated by Massachusetts Bay Commuter Railroad struck a track maintenance vehicle that was on the track near Woburn, Massachusetts. The track maintenance vehicle was thrown forward about 210 feet; the train did not derail. Of the six maintenance-of-way employees working on or near the track maintenance vehicle, two were killed, and two were seriously injured. Emergency responders treated and released 10 passengers at the accident scene.

As a result of its investigation of the accident, the National Transportation Safety Board identified the following safety issues: train dispatcher procedures for blocking track segments to protect maintenance-of-way work crews working on the track; maintenance-of-way work crews shunting signaled track to protect themselves while working on the track; and alcohol and drug use by maintenance-of-way employees in the railroad industry

As a result of its investigation of this accident, the National Transportation Safety Board makes recommendations to the Federal Railroad Administration and the Brotherhood of Maintenance of Way Employes Division.

CONTENTS

ACRONYMS AND ABBREVIATIONS

Amtrak	National Railroad Passenger Corporation
CFR	*Code of Federal Regulations*
FRA	Federal Railroad Administration
MBCR	Massachusetts Bay Commuter Railroad
MBTA	Massachusetts Bay Transportation Authority
NORAC	Northeast Operating Rules Advisory Committee

EXECUTIVE SUMMARY

On Tuesday, January 9, 2007, at 1:38 p.m., southbound Massachusetts Bay Transportation Authority passenger train 322 operated by Massachusetts Bay Commuter Railroad struck a track maintenance vehicle that was on the track near Woburn, Massachusetts. Passenger train 322 consisted of six passenger cars, including a lead control car, and a locomotive pushing from the rear. The track maintenance vehicle was thrown forward about 210 feet; the train did not derail. Of the six maintenance-of-way employees working on or near the track maintenance vehicle, two were killed, and two were seriously injured. Emergency responders treated and released 10 passengers at the accident scene.

As a result of the accident, 160 feet of rail, 80 crossties, and 100 tons of ballast had to be replaced. The cost, including labor, was $15,841. The accident damaged the lead control car and undercarriage of the train. Repairing the train cost an estimated $450,000. The track maintenance vehicle was destroyed; replacing it cost $95,000. Total estimated property damage was $560,841.

The National Transportation Safety Board determines that the probable cause of the January 9, 2007, collision of train 322 with a track maintenance vehicle near Woburn, Massachusetts, was the failure of the train dispatcher to maintain blocking that provided signal protection for the track segment occupied by the maintenance-of-way work crew, and the failure of the work crew to apply a shunting device that would have provided redundant signal protection for their track segment. Contributing to the accident was Massachusetts Bay Commuter Railroad's failure to ensure that maintenance-of-way work crews applied shunting devices as required.

As a result of its investigation of the accident, the National Transportation Safety Board identified the following safety issues:

- Train dispatcher procedures for blocking track segments to protect maintenance-of-way work crews working on the track
- Maintenance-of-way work crews shunting signaled track to protect themselves while working on the track
- Alcohol and drug use by maintenance-of-way employees in the railroad industry

As a result of its investigation of this accident, the National Transportation Safety Board makes recommendations to the Federal Railroad Administration and the Brotherhood of Maintenance of Way Employes Division.

FACTUAL INFORMATION

Accident Synopsis

On Tuesday, January 9, 2007, at 1:38 p.m.,[1] southbound Massachusetts Bay Transportation Authority (MBTA) passenger train 322 operated by Massachusetts Bay Commuter Railroad (MBCR) struck a track maintenance vehicle that was on the track near Woburn, Massachusetts. Passenger train 322 consisted of six passenger cars, including a lead control car, and a locomotive pushing from the rear. The track maintenance vehicle was thrown forward about 210 feet; the train did not derail. Of the six maintenance-of-way employees (work crew) working on or near the track maintenance vehicle, two were killed, and two were seriously injured. Emergency responders treated and released 10 passengers at the accident scene.

As a result of the accident, 160 feet of rail, 80 crossties, and 100 tons of ballast had to be replaced. The cost, including labor, was $15,841. The accident damaged the lead control car and undercarriage of the train. Repairing the train cost an estimated $450,000. The track maintenance vehicle was destroyed; replacing it cost $95,000. Total estimated damage was $560,841.

Accident Narrative

Preaccident Events

On the day of the accident, the track crew went on duty at Wilmington, Massachusetts, at 7:30 a.m.[2] The supervisor told the track crew foreman to replace crossties near the Woburn industrial switch on track 2. To accomplish this work, the track crew needed a track maintenance vehicle—a speed swing[3]—to lift the ties that were to be replaced. (See figure 1.) The foreman told the operator of the track maintenance vehicle to drive it to Rothstein's switch, where it could be easily placed on track 2. The rest of the track crew gathered the necessary tools and supplies and met the operator at Rothstein's switch about 9:30 a.m.

---

[1] All times in this report are eastern standard time.

[2] All times in this report are rounded to the nearest minute.

[3] A *speed swing* is an on-track maintenance vehicle that uses a hook to lift railroad crossties.

Figure 1. Pettibone Speed Swing 445E.[4]

The train dispatcher gave the foreman authority to occupy track 2 between Crawford and Winchester. (See figure 2.) At 9:45 a.m., the track segment between Crawford and Winchester had been designated "out of service" on a Form D track permit, which also said, "clear track by 3:00 p.m." When the dispatcher authorized the track permit, the dispatching system recorded the track segment as "blocked," meaning that the track signals controlling entry displayed a red aspect, which is a *stop* indication for approaching trains. The crewmembers put the track maintenance vehicle on their track segment and proceeded to the work location, where they began replacing crossties. A watchman was assigned to warn the track crew of trains that were approaching on the adjacent track (track 1).

In the meantime, a track inspector had asked for and received permission from the foreman to operate a hy-rail inspection truck through the track crew's work area[5] on track 2. The dispatcher verified with the foreman that the inspector had the foreman's permission. The inspector started about noon, when the track crew was at lunch and, thus, clear of the track. The track maintenance vehicle operator, who was eating lunch in the cab of the machine, said that he saw the hy-rail inspection truck pass the work area.

---

[4] The Speed Swing 445E was built by Pettibone. It had four large rubber tractor tires and was equipped with steel wheels that could be lowered onto the rail. The Speed Swing had a hydraulically powered front arm with several different attachments. On the day of the accident, it was equipped for handling crossties. The machine weighed 32,217 pounds.

[5] Under the MBCR's Special Instructions, 133-S2, an inspector can enter and/or travel on an out-of-service track segment as authorization is received from the foreman who "controls" the track.

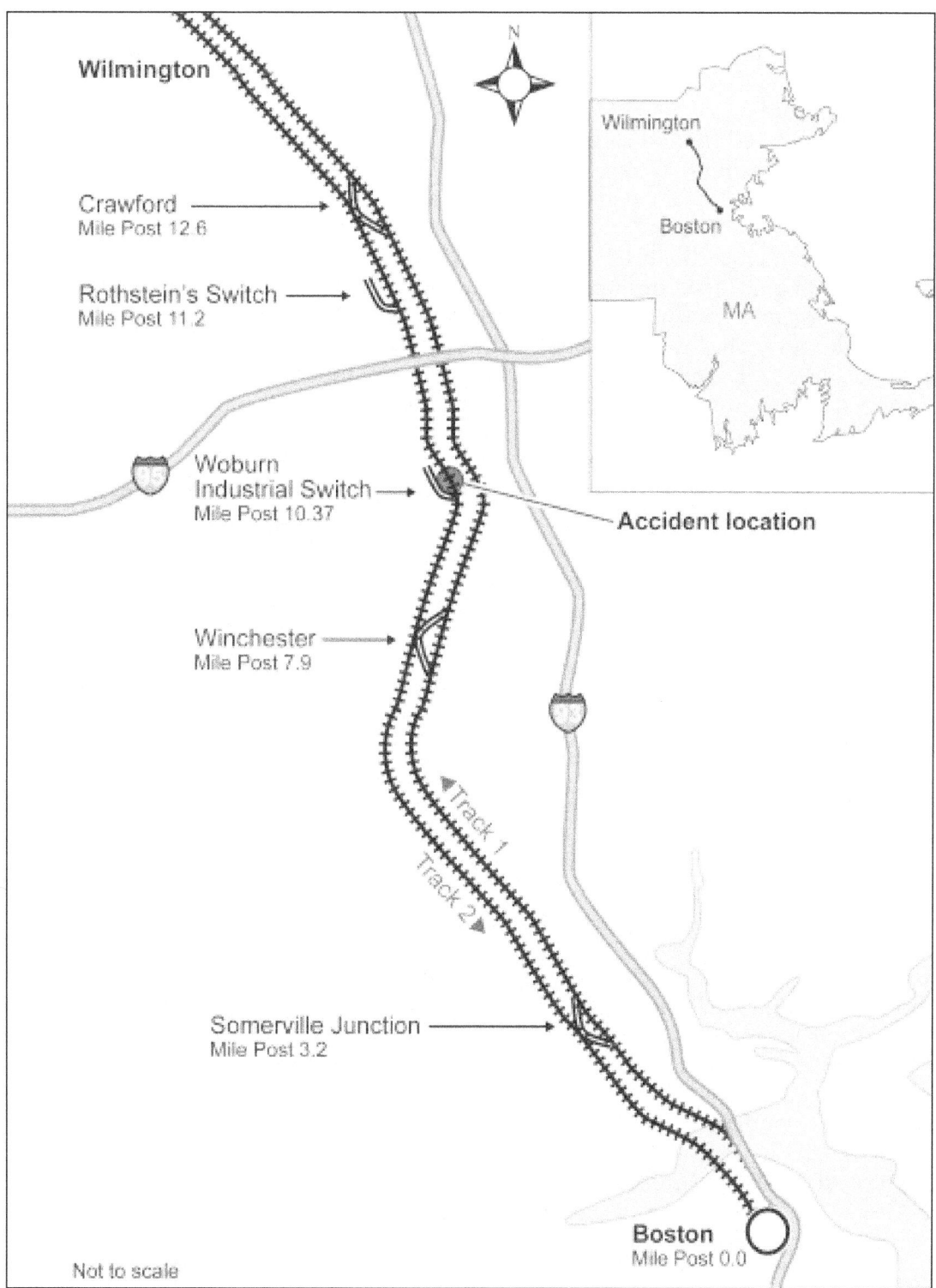

Figure 2. Map of accident area.

At 12:46 p.m., the track inspector reached Winchester and asked the dispatcher for the authority to enter the track segment between Winchester and Somerville Junction. The dispatcher placed a block on the track segment and then authorized the track inspector to proceed. The inspector stopped at Somerville Junction; he asked for and received permission from the dispatcher to pass the red signal at Somerville Junction. After the inspector passed Somerville Junction, he told the dispatcher that he had departed the track segment between Winchester and Somerville Junction. At 1:25 p.m., the dispatcher formally acknowledged his report; she did not unblock the track segment that he had just released. About 5 minutes later, at 1:30 p.m., according to the dispatching system,[6] the dispatcher unblocked the track segment between Crawford and Winchester, the segment occupied by the track crew. The track segment between Winchester and Somerville Junction that had been released by the track inspector remained blocked. At 1:32 p.m., the dispatcher cleared the signal at Crawford that allowed entry into the track segment from Crawford to Winchester by a southbound train.[7] At 1:37 p.m., southbound train 322 entered the track segment from Crawford to Winchester. However, the track segment had been removed from service and the track maintenance crew had been given exclusive track occupancy, so their expectation was that no train would be permitted on the track while they were working on it. Trains would be allowed to pass on the adjacent track, and a watchman was provided to alert the maintenance crew of any passing trains so the crew would remain clear of the adjacent track.

Collision

Event recorder data from train 322 indicates that the engineer initiated emergency braking at 62 mph and the train speed decreased to approximately 44 mph at the time of the collision. In postaccident interviews, the engineer said that his last signal indication was clear and, as he exited the curve, he noted equipment on his track. He sounded the whistle and put his train into emergency, but was unable to stop before striking the vehicle.

The watchman told investigators that he looked north and saw the approaching train. He blew his handheld compressed air warning horn and started yelling at the other crewmembers. The track maintenance vehicle operator started blowing the whistle on his machinery when he heard the watchman's horn (a normal practice when a train approaches on an adjacent track). He then looked in the rear view mirrors and realized the train was on his track. He opened the door of the track maintenance vehicle and jumped to the ground. He recalled seeing the crewmembers who were killed standing in front of the track maintenance vehicle before it was struck. About 1:39 p.m., the train engineer radioed the dispatcher

---

[6] The dispatching system records the time when the dispatcher sends a message to request a field device to change its status and then records the time when a message is received from the device indicating that the change has occurred.

[7] At 1:33 p.m., according to the dispatching system, the dispatcher unblocked the track segment from Winchester to Somerville Junction.

that he had just hit some track equipment. (See figure 3.) Shortly thereafter, an audio recording recorded the train dispatcher saying that she had pulled down (that is, removed) the wrong block.

Figure 3. Damaged track maintenance vehicle.

Injuries

Of the six track employees working on or near the track maintenance vehicle, the track foreman and the track worker/welder were killed. The assistant foreman and the track maintenance vehicle operator were seriously injured. The remaining two track workers were not injured. Emergency responders treated and released 10 passengers at the accident scene.

Damage

As a result of the accident, 160 feet of rail, 80 crossties, and 100 tons of ballast had to be replaced. The cost, including labor, was $15,841. The accident damaged the lead control car and the undercarriage of the train. Repairing the train cost an estimated $450,000. The track maintenance vehicle was destroyed; replacing it cost $95,000. The total estimated damage was $560,841.

Personnel Information

The MBTA owned the railroad where the accident occurred. However, it contracted out the operations, equipment maintenance, and track maintenance. The MBCR became the contractor in 2003, and on the day of the accident, all of the railroad employees, including supervisors, train dispatchers, train crew, and maintenance-of-way employees, were MBCR employees.

The operating company for the railroad changed from the Boston and Maine Railroad to Gilford Transportation Industries (1983), to Amtrak (1986), and then to the MBCR (2003). The foreman and machine operator had been hired by the Boston and Maine Railroad and stayed in the Boston area working for each of the different railroads. The rest of the employees had started working for the railroad under Amtrak. The information available in the current MBCR personnel files is primarily from between 2003 and the date of the accident. The foreman and other track workers typically worked from 7:30 a.m. to 3:30 p.m., Monday through Friday. The train dispatcher did not have a fixed schedule but worked when called to duty.

Foreman

The 54-year-old track foreman was killed in the accident. He had been hired by the Boston and Maine Railroad on September 12, 1977. He had started as a trackman and worked through the normal job progression, training, and examinations to become a qualified foreman. He had not worked during the weekend. He had worked a normal shift on Monday, and he had started his shift on the day of the accident at 7:00 a.m.

Assistant Foreman

The 51-year-old assistant track foreman was seriously injured. He had been hired by Amtrak on October 26, 1988. He had started as a trackman and worked through the normal job progression to become a qualified foreman.

Machine Operator

The 55-year-old machine operator had been hired by the Boston and Maine Railroad on August 25, 1975. He had started as a trackman and worked through the normal job progression to become a qualified machine operator. He was injured when he jumped from the track maintenance vehicle.

Second Machine Operator

The 54-year-old second machine operator had been hired by Amtrak on September 6, 1997. He had started as a trackman and worked through the normal job progression to become a qualified machine operator. He was working on the ground at the time of the accident and was not injured.

Welder/Watchman

The 37-year-old welder had been hired by Amtrak on December 5, 1994. He had started as a truck driver and later qualified for a welder position. He was working as a watchman on the day of the accident and was not injured.

Track Worker/Welder

The 30-year-old track worker/welder was killed in the accident. He had been hired by Amtrak on January 3, 1995. He had started as a trackman and later qualified as a welder. He was working on the track on the day of the accident.

Train Dispatcher

The 31-year-old train dispatcher had been hired by Amtrak on January 17, 2002. She had established a seniority date on February 18, 2002, working a customer service desk. She received on-the-job training under the supervision of a qualified train dispatcher. In May 2002, she qualified to work the Boston East dispatching desk. In May 2003, she had qualified to work the Boston West dispatching desk (the desk for the territory where the accident occurred). On the Sunday before the accident, she had worked from 7:00 a.m. to 3:00 p.m. On Monday, she had been on call but had not worked. She said that she had just sat around her apartment and had gone to bed about 9:30 p.m. or 10:00 p.m. and that she had felt rested when she started working on Tuesday at 7:00 a.m.

Signal System

Train movements were authorized by signal indications of a traffic control system on the wayside of each track segment. The signals were controlled and monitored by the MBCR's dispatching office in Somerville, Massachusetts.

Maintenance-of-Way Procedures

Train movements in the area where the accident occurred were authorized by a dispatcher at the MBCR's operation center in Somerville, Massachusetts. At the time of the accident, train movements were under the *Northeast Operating Rules Advisory Committee Rulebook* (8th Edition, effective January 1, 2003). The rulebook was supplemented by the following:

- MBCR Service Employee Timetable No. 5, effective April 24, 2006
- General Order No. 501, effective January 1, 2006
- General Order No. 502, effective April 24, 2006
- *Train Dispatcher's Manual*, effective January 1, 2006.

According to the rulebook, a maintenance-of-way foreman must get a Form D Track Permit Line 4 authorization from the dispatcher before placing equipment on a track. The permit removes the track segment from service and puts it under the control of the foreman. This action creates an "exclusive track occupancy" for the track crew; therefore, no train is allowed on the crew's track segment.

Rule 133-S1, Protection of Out-Of-Service Track (a supplemental instruction in the Service Employee Timetable No. 5), requires the employee-in-charge to place "… a shunting barricade at each end of the work area within the Line 4 limits." The shunting barricade used by the MBCR consists of a shunting device and a metal flag referred to as a barricade. The metal flag (barricade) does not physically restrict train movement, but it does provide a visual warning that the track segment is occupied. The shunting device provides an electrical connection between the rails and indicates to the signal system that the track is occupied, so that the signals at the entrance to the segment cannot be cleared. When a track is shunted, the signals display the most restrictive indication, as though a train is occupying the track.

The dispatcher cannot clear signal indications for trains approaching a block that is occupied by another train. Therefore, if a train dispatcher makes a mistake, the train's track occupancy still provides signal protection. Many vehicles used for railroad maintenance (such as the equipment used on the day of the accident) have been modified to operate on railroad tracks. However, unlike a train, track maintenance equipment operating on track seldom shunts the track. Consequently, if a dispatcher makes a mistake, nothing provides signal protection for a track maintenance crew unless a shunting device has been applied.

According to the track inspector, the shunts were not in place when he inspected the track before the accident. When one of the track crewmembers was asked whether shunts had been used, he could not remember. However, when he was asked to remember the last time he had seen a track shunted, he replied

> It's been a while, because we, really, basically – it's only when we have the big, big jobs. When you have big jobs when you did that, not like regular maintenance jobs or just maintenance work, because we always had to flag them.

Interviews with track maintenance employees, including those not involved in the accident, confirmed that it was common practice to use shunts only for big jobs and that replacing ties, as the track crew in the accident had been doing, was considered to be a small job. During the investigation, MBCR's track supervisors did not have specific records indicating whether shunting devices were used for all track maintenance jobs.

Train Dispatching

When an MBCR dispatcher blocks a track segment, a computer entry is required to identify for whom the segment is being blocked. At the time of the accident, the dispatcher could enter one of the following into the computer: the name of the foreman, the number of the track gang, the number of the equipment, or the number of the track permit. The accident dispatcher chose the track permit number and entered *M302*.

A dispatcher unblocks a track segment by selecting it on the computer screen, viewing the onscreen information that identifies the recipient of the blocked track, and then unblocking the track segment.

Each track segment on a train dispatcher's computer screen is color-coded. A white segment is unoccupied. A green segment is unoccupied and has been cleared by the dispatcher for an approaching train movement. A red segment is occupied, by either a train or a shunt. A blue segment has been blocked by the train dispatcher. A magenta segment is both blocked (blue) and occupied (red). While the Track Permit was in effect, the dispatcher computer data log shows that the segment turned from blue to magenta only twice. The first time was at 10:41 a.m. for 18 minutes; the second time was at 1:14 p.m. for 8 minutes.

Management Oversight

The MBCR monitors the effectiveness of and compliance with its operating rules by field audits, using its Program of Operational Tests and Inspections (effective July 1, 2003, and revised July 1, 2005).

The Program defines "Tests" and "Observations" as follows:

A "Test" is a rules compliance check, which requires an active effort on the part of the supervisor or supervisors, and includes an action on the part of the employee being tested. Examples would include conducting a question-and-answer session with a train crew to determine rules familiarity or conducting restricted signal tests in conjunction with a train dispatcher and/or signal maintainer. An "Observation" is distinguished from a

"Test" in that an observation is the passive monitoring of an employee, either observed or unobserved, in the normal course of his/her duties, by a supervisor.

According to the MBCR's records from July 1, 2003, to January 9, 2007, the maintenance-of-way employees and the dispatcher had been observed.[8] The foreman had been observed while performing his duties by a supervisor on 67 occasions in the 3 years preceding the accident. On 13 occasions, the foreman had been observed for use of drugs or alcohol; all of his observations were negative. His most recent observation had been on December 28, 2006. The MBCR was unable to provide specific records indicating that the foreman had been observed for compliance with rule 140-S2, which outlines the steps to be taken when a track is taken out of service. One of these steps requires the employee-in-charge (in this case, the foreman) to confirm that the track is shunted. The track foreman had passed the annual exams for the *Roadway Worker Protection* (consisting of 25 questions) and the *Northeast Operating Rules Advisory Committee (NORAC) Operating Rules* (consisting of 50 questions).

The train dispatcher had been observed while performing her duties by a supervisor on 53 occasions in the 3 years preceding the accident. Three rule non-compliances were noted on the same day in 2005: two radio uses and one procedural issue. During the other 50 observations, 5 of which were "applying and removing" blocking devices, she properly followed the rules and procedures.

The train dispatcher had passed the required initial examinations: *NORAC Operating Rules Blocking Device Examination For New Hire Dispatchers And Operators* (consisting of 20 questions) and *Operating Rules Examination For New Train Dispatchers* (consisting of 100 questions). She also had passed the annual rules examination (consisting of 50 questions). Her records show that she had correctly answered the questions regarding blocking procedures.

Toxicological Testing

Under Federal regulations, the engineer, conductor, assistant conductor, and train dispatcher are defined as "covered" employees[9] and are required in 49 *Code of Federal Regulations* (CFR) 219.203 (a)(1) by the Federal Railroad Administration (FRA) to provide specimens for postaccident toxicological testing. These four covered employees provided specimens, and all test results were negative for alcohol and drugs.[10]

---

[8] Although the records indicated that no tests were performed, the MBCR indicated that it believed that tests had been performed but that the information had been entered improperly as observations (instead of tests) in the database.

[9] Title 49 CFR 219.5 states, "*Covered employee* means a person who has been assigned to perform service in the United States subject to the hours of service laws..."

[10] These substances include cannabinoids, cocaine, opiates, phencyclidine, amphetamines, barbiturates, and benzodiazepines.

Under Federal regulations, track workers are "non-covered" employees and are not subject to most of the alcohol and drug testing requirements. However, postaccident testing of the remains of non-covered employees who are fatally injured in train accidents and incidents is required in 49 CFR 219.203 (a) (4). The surviving non-covered employees are not subject to postaccident testing under Federal authority. Consequently, the remains of the track foreman and the track worker/welder were tested, and the four surviving track workers were not tested.

The track worker/welder's test results were negative for alcohol and drugs. The foreman's test results were negative for alcohol but positive for cannabinoids. The concentrations of tetrahydrocannabinol and tetrahydrocannabinol carboxylic acid in his blood were 16.9 nanograms per milliliter (ng/ml) and 40.0 ng/ml, respectively.

Previous Board Action: Alcohol and Drug Testing

Over the years, the Safety Board has made recommendations concerning alcohol and drug use by transportation workers in safety-sensitive positions. In 1987, the Safety Board undertook a safety study[11] to review the first full year of implementation of the FRA's alcohol and drug testing rules. The rules established requirements for postaccident toxicological testing and testing for cause. Random alcohol and drug testing was not required at that time.[12] The rules applied to only certain covered (hours-of-service) employees, such as dispatchers, signalmen, engineers, conductors, and others on trains. The rules did not apply to maintenance-of-way employees, maintenance-of-equipment employees, or others in safety-sensitive positions.[13]

As a result of the safety study, the Safety Board issued 11 recommendations to the FRA. One of those recommendations is relevant to the alcohol and drug use issue that has arisen again in the Woburn investigation:

> R-88-23
>
> Amend 49 CFR Part 219 to require postaccident toxicological testing of all employees in safety-sensitive positions.

The FRA responded on September 21, 1990, to the Safety Board that it had reviewed this issue on several occasions and concluded that employees covered

---

[11] See National Transportation Safety Board, *Alcohol/Drug Use and Its Impact on Railroad Safety,* Safety Study NTSB/SS-88/04 (Washington, DC: NTSB, 1988).

[12] In a subsequent rule, the FRA established a requirement for random alcohol and drug testing of covered service employees commencing on November 21, 1989.

[13] Safety-sensitive functions are defined in 49 CFR Part 209.303.

by the Hours of Service Act occupy the most safety-sensitive positions on the railroads and are the proper focus of Federal requirements. The FRA stated,

> Categorical expansion of those tested following accidents would either result in an excessive testing burden in relation to the benefits derived (e.g., testing of an entire track gang at the scene of a derailment) or in an overboard delegation of decisional authority to the railroad supervisor in the field.

In subsequent correspondence on March 3, 1994, the FRA again stated that it found no basis to expand postaccident toxicological testing to other railroad crafts. On May 3, 1994, the Safety Board replied,

> Based on FRA's response, the Safety Board classifies Safety Recommendation R-88-23 "Closed — Reconsidered." However, the Safety Board will continue to monitor this issue closely.

Postaccident Actions

MBCR

Following the accident, the MBCR implemented various new instructions and procedures affecting the performance of the maintenance-of-way employees and train dispatchers. Programs were also started to enhance the communication between the railroad and the Brotherhood of Maintenance of Way Employes Division.

The MBCR issued the following items that specifically address improving safety for the employees occupying the track while performing work:

- Train Dispatcher Notice Number 07-01 requires the train dispatcher to overlay an additional block in the dispatching system if additional equipment is authorized to enter out-of-service track. Further, it requires that the foreman's name be entered in the dialogue box that is used to identify for whom the blocking is applied.

- Supplemental Bulletin Order No. 5-56A has new, more specific instructions for maintenance-of-way employees who are shunting a track after receiving authority to occupy a track segment. The instructions require the shunting to be verified by the train dispatcher or a qualified signal employee to ensure that the signals protecting the work area can display only restrictive indications.

- Supplemental Bulletin Order No. 5-57A provides procedures to be used so that the signals leading to work areas display the most restrictive indication when maintenance-of-way employees are in the work area for more than 30 minutes.

- Special Instruction 905-S1 requires verbal verification between the train dispatcher and the foreman. The train dispatcher must verify that blocking devices have been applied, and the foreman must specify the type of protection that will be utilized in the work area.

- The Roadway Worker Protection training program was enhanced by adding specific instructions to the program and by adding training that addresses protection while working on the track.

- Managers were told to focus their tests and observations on safety-critical rules, procedures, and special instructions that include but are not limited to the following: supplemental protection, Form D compliance, On Track Safety compliance, Rule G compliance, lock out/tag out compliance, movement permit compliance, job briefings, removing tracks from service, and radio procedures.

- The MBCR re-launched Operation Red Block[14] on April 2, 2007, to coincide with alcohol and drug awareness month. A steering committee has been formed; it consists of the director of safety, chief transportation officer, and 18 union representatives. Thirty-two peer captains are presently in place system-wide. One employee was selected and has been licensed to handle evaluations. Red Block representatives have visited many of the on-duty locations to introduce the program to the employees.

Safety Compliance Agreement

On January 26 and February 5, 2007, MBCR's General Manager and staff met with regional FRA employees to discuss development of a Safety Compliance Agreement with the agency. On May 29, 2007, the FRA, the MBTA, and the MBCR adopted the final version of the Safety Compliance Agreement (the Agreement).

The Agreement includes background information about the circumstances that led to the need for such an agreement. Between December 2003 and January 2007, the MBCR had four fatalities, one critical injury, and one potentially serious incident involving MBCR maintenance-of-way employees. According to the Agreement, these accidents involved violations of railroad operating rules and/or Federal Roadway Worker Protection regulations (49 CFR Part 214), although the carrier makes no admission of violation. The Agreement also states that as a result of these incidents, seven maintenance-of-way employees were tested for drugs and/or alcohol. The four fatally injured employees were tested under Federal

---

[14] Operation Red Block is a labor-developed, company-adopted alcohol and drug prevention and interception program that emphasizes awareness of, education about, and prevention of alcohol and drug use through union-led prevention committees. Operation Red Block started in 1983.

authority, and the three surviving employees were tested at the request of the company. The background information in the Agreement states, "Of that number [seven], four employees tested positive, and one employee submitted a specimen that may have masked a positive (negative dilute)."

The Agreement details future MBCR actions in the following three major areas: (1) compliance with roadway worker protection, (2) compliance with the FRA's regulations on railroad operating rules, and (3) actions to be undertaken regarding control of alcohol and drug use.

Regarding compliance with the Roadway Worker Protection Program, the Agreement asks for the following actions:

> Train the train dispatchers on the Roadway Worker Protection Program; establish procedures to monitor the effectiveness of and compliance with the on-track safety program; establish procedures to record all authorities issued for exclusive track occupancy; require verbal communication between the train dispatcher and the track foremen when working limits are established — specifically include the application/removal of blocking devices and application/removal of the protection applied in the field (that is, barricade shunting); provide to the FRA records of the employees qualified on the Roadway Worker Protection Program; conduct training for roadway workers, train dispatchers, and supervisors of both working groups on the application of shunting barricades, other field protection methods, Form D requirements, and the application and removal of blocking devices; provide to the FRA a description of the procedures and of the "good-faith challenge"[15] by an employee concerning an on-track safety provision; and train the employees on the procedures of a good-faith challenge.

Regarding compliance with the FRA's regulations, the Agreement specified the following actions: provide to the FRA the current Operational Testing Program, re-instruct supervisors on the Operational Testing Program, perform a monthly analysis of the efficacy of the Operational Testing Program, perform an internal audit of the Operational Testing Program, and designate by name or title an employee directly responsible for the implementation of the Operational Testing Program.

Regarding alcohol and drug concerns, the Agreement identified the following actions: provide supplemental training for the supervisors on signs and symptoms of alcohol and drug influence, make a good faith effort to work with the applicable parties to institute a company random testing program of maintenance-of-way employees, invigorate the Red Block program, and implement a plan to increase observations for alcohol and drug use by maintenance-of-way employees.

---

[15] Title 49 CFR Part 214.311, *Responsibility of employers*, (b): Each employer shall guarantee each employee the absolute right to challenge in good faith whether the on-track safety procedures to be applied at the job location comply with the rules of the operating railroad, and to remain clear of the track until the challenge is resolved.

ANALYSIS

Exclusions

Safety Board investigators reviewed the signal system data logs. Signal system data indicated that the signals were functioning properly at the time of the accident. Investigators interviewed the train crew. The crew stated that the signals appeared normal and the response of the equipment was typical on the day of the accident. The Safety Board concludes that the signal system performance and the train engineer's performance were not factors in this accident.

Train Dispatching

After the track inspector reported that he was clear of the track segment between Winchester and Somerville Junction on track 2, the train dispatcher erroneously removed the blocking from the segment where the track crew was working (between Crawford and Winchester), not the segment just recently vacated by the track inspector (between Winchester and Somerville Junction). Moments later, when the train dispatcher needed to move southbound train 322, track 2 was not blocked at Crawford. She then set the signals to allow train 322 to enter the track segment between Crawford and Winchester. Train 322 entered the track segment on a clear signal indication and was unable to stop before striking the track crew. The train engineer initiated emergency braking, and train speed decreased from 62 mph to approximately 44 mph at the time of the collision. After the engineer reported the collision, the dispatcher was recorded saying that she had pulled down (that is, removed) the wrong block.

Normally, the train dispatcher would have unblocked the track segment between Winchester and Somerville Junction after the track inspector reported that he had cleared that segment; however, the dispatching system recorded that she actually unblocked the segment where the track crew was working. Therefore, the Safety Board concludes that the train dispatcher forgot about the maintenance-of-way work crew and removed the blocking from the wrong track segment, allowing train 322 to enter the work area on a clear signal indication.

Since the accident, the MBCR has changed the required entries for the dispatching computer system. The train dispatcher must now enter the name of each individual for whom the track segment has been blocked. In this accident, the train dispatcher used the track permit number to identify the track crew. Therefore, when the dispatcher unblocked the track segment, the dialogue box on the computer screen displayed a number rather than the name of the individual who had received the authority for the track segment. Had the dispatcher used the foreman's name to block the track, she would have seen that the name of the track inspector did not match the name of the foreman, and that should have alerted her before she unblocked the wrong track segment.

Further, the MBCR has added the requirement that a second movement into a territory (in this case, the track inspector's) must also be entered into the computer dispatching system. At the time of the accident, only one entry was required. If the new requirement had been in effect on the day of the accident, the names of both the foreman and the track inspector would have been entered into the computer dispatching system for the track between Crawford and Winchester. To remove the blocking, the dispatcher would have had to remove both names from the system.

The primary method used by railroads to protect roadway workers with exclusive track occupancy is by train dispatcher blocking and unblocking of track segments. The layers of redundant steps required for the dispatcher to block and unblock track segments vary from railroad to railroad depending on their procedures and the design of their dispatching system. Although the MBCR has modified its dispatching methods since this accident, the potential exists on other railroads for a dispatcher to incorrectly apply or remove the protection. Therefore, the Safety Board recommends that the FRA advise railroads of the need to examine their train dispatching systems and procedures to ensure that appropriate safety redundancies are in place for establishing protection and preventing undesired removal of protection for roadway workers receiving track occupancy authority.

Track Maintenance Activities

On the day of the accident, the track segment had been removed from service and the track maintenance crew had been given exclusive track occupancy; so their expectation was that no train would be permitted on the track while they were working on it. However, trains would be allowed to pass on the adjacent track, and a watchman was provided to alert the maintenance crew of passing trains.

The watchman told investigators that he blew his handheld warning horn after seeing the approaching train and that he also yelled at the other crewmembers. The track maintenance vehicle operator started blowing the whistle on his machinery when he heard the watchman's horn in order to repeat the warning of a train on an adjacent track. However, the vehicle operator said that when he looked into his rear view mirrors, he realized that the train was actually approaching on the same track and he jumped from his vehicle just before the impact. The vehicle operator also stated that as he jumped he saw the crewmembers who were killed standing in front of the track maintenance vehicle just before it was struck by the train.

The train engineer had a clear signal indication and did not have any knowledge that a track maintenance crew would be occupying the same track. After exiting a curve at approximately 62 mph, little time (about 15 seconds) was available before the train reached the work area. The engineer realized that the work crew was on his track and initiated emergency braking. Train speed decreased to approximately 44 mph at the time of the collision.

A shunting device electrically prevents the signals from displaying clear indications to approaching trains. When the track inspector drove through the track segment occupied by the track maintenance crew, he did not encounter a shunting device. The train dispatcher also could not recall the track being color-coded magenta on the dispatching computer screen. Had the work crew shunted the segment of track, the dispatcher's screen would have displayed magenta for the entire time the work crew was at that location. On the day of the accident, the dispatcher computer data log showed the track being shunted only twice: one time for 18 minutes, and later for 8 minutes. The relatively brief recorded shunts were likely a result of the incidental actions by the work crew (such as moving tools or equipment or opening a switch), not of an intentional shunting. The Safety Board concludes that the maintenance-of-way work crew did not apply a shunting device; therefore, additional signal protection did not exist for the track segment they occupied, and the dispatcher's screen did not indicate the track segment was occupied.

MBCR rules required the track foreman to have a shunting device at each end of the work area every time a track was taken out-of-service for maintenance. However, interviews with track maintenance employees, including those not involved in the accident, confirmed that it was common practice to use shunting devices only for big jobs and that replacing ties, as the track crew in the accident had been doing, was considered to be a small job. The track crew had reserved the track segment from 9:45 a.m. to 3:00 p.m. and was clearly engaged in a significant amount of work on the day of the accident. The Safety Board concludes that MBCR maintenance-of-way work crews routinely reduced safety by not using shunting devices when performing jobs that required the track to be out of service.

The MBCR had many opportunities to be aware that the requirement to use shunting devices was commonly disregarded. For example, track supervisors visiting work sites could have seen that a shunting device (and attached metal flag) was not used as required. Transportation supervisors on passing trains could have observed that shunting devices were not in place. Dispatching supervisors could have noted the absence of a magenta indication on the dispatching screens. Finally, MBCR's program of tests and observations should have provided a safety net to ensure that compliance with Rule 140-S2 was frequently examined. The Safety Board concludes that the MBCR's management failed to ensure that maintenance-of-way work crews were using shunting devices as required.

Since the accident, supervisors at the MBCR have focused their tests and observations on safety-critical rules procedures, including On Track Safety compliance. According to MBCR data from July 1, 2007, to November 1, 2007, supervisors observed track employees removing track from service 35 times. In all instances, the employees properly applied a shunt.

The Safety Compliance Agreement, which followed the accident, addresses the need for better communication regarding the train dispatcher's blocking procedures and an employee's shunting in the field. Further, the Agreement specifies the training of employees and the observational testing of employees by supervisors. As a postaccident action, the MBCR is emphasizing its requirement that the track be shunted with verification by either a train dispatcher or a qualified signal employee to ensure that the signals cannot be cleared for trains approaching the work area.

The Safety Board is aware that shunting by track maintenance work crews on main track is not a common practice in the railroad industry. This may be due, in large part, to the absence of a Federal requirement for shunting to provide maintenance-of-way work crew protection. Unless a shunting device is used by the work crew, the train dispatcher provides the only signal protection in controlled territory. As this accident demonstrates, the dispatching system is not immune to human error, and electrically shunting the rails is therefore an important safety redundancy. The Safety Board concludes that maintenance-of-way work crews on all railroads who depend on the train dispatcher for signal protection need redundant protection to restrict train movements into work areas. Therefore, the Safety Board recommends that the FRA require redundant signal protection, such as shunting, for maintenance-of-way work crews who depend on the train dispatcher to provide signal protection.

Alcohol/Drug Use by Maintenance-of-Way Employees

The fatally injured track foreman tested positive[16] for marijuana. An analysis of the levels of tetrahydrocannibinol and tetrahydrocannabinol carboxylic acid in the foreman's blood suggest that he had likely used marijuana within 3 hours of his death and possibly much more recently.[17] The most likely opportunity for his marijuana use was when the work crew broke for lunch, from about noon to 1:00 p.m.

Marijuana can have a number of psychomotor effects on human performance, including ataxia, confusion, dizziness, somnolence, speech difficulties, weakness,

---

[16] The FRA toxicology report indicates tetrahydrocannibinol, the psychoactive substance in marijuana, at a level of 16.9 ng/ml and tetrahydrocannabinol carboxylic acid, an inactive metabolite of marijuana, at a level of 40 ng/ml in the foreman's blood.

[17] Based on data in: M.A. Huestis, J.E. Henningfield, and E.J. Cone, "Blood cannabinoids. II. Models for the Prediction of Time of Marijuana Exposure from Plasma Concentrations of Δ^9-Tetrahydrocannabinol (THC) and 11-nor-9-carboxy-Δ^9-tetrahydrocannabinol (THCCOOH)," *Journal of Analytical Toxicology*, 1992 Sep–Oct;16(5):283–90.

and vision difficulties. Studies clearly demonstrate impairment of driving-related skills up to 3 hours after the use of marijuana.[18] The Safety Board concludes that the foreman's performance would likely have been measurably impaired at the time of the accident by his recent use of marijuana.

The positive drug test result for the track foreman is not an isolated incident among MBCR maintenance-of-way employees. The Safety Compliance Agreement discusses four MBCR accidents within a 3-year period (December 2003 – January 2007) involving maintenance-of-way employees. Following these accidents, seven maintenance-of-way employees were tested for alcohol and/or drugs. Four of the employees were fatally injured and therefore were tested under Federal authority. Two of the four fatalities tested positive and are included in the FRA postaccident test data described later in this section. The three surviving employees were tested at company request; consequently, they are not included in the FRA postaccident test data. Two of the survivors tested positive, and the third survivor submitted a diluted specimen that may have masked a positive.

The fact that a majority of the employees had positive test results is symptomatic of a substance abuse problem among MBCR's maintenance-of-way employees. The FRA addressed this problem in the Safety Compliance Agreement by prescribing multiple actions, including having the MBCR make a good faith effort to work with the applicable parties to institute a company random alcohol and drug testing program of maintenance-of-way employees.

The MBCR's percentage of positive test results involving maintenance-of-way employees in postaccident alcohol and drug testing is a cause for concern. The Safety Board also reviewed industry-wide postaccident test data for accidents involving maintenance-of-way employee fatalities. Postaccident test data provided to the Board by the FRA show that over the 10-year period ending January 9, 2007, (the date of this accident) the postaccident testing of 26 maintenance-of-way fatalities resulted in 5 positive test results, a 19.23 percent positive rate. The positive rate for maintenance-of-way employees is in marked contrast to the postaccident test results of covered employees. During the same 10-year period, FRA postaccident test data for accidents involving 122 fatally injured covered employees show 8 positive test results, a 6.56 percent positive rate. Covered employees are subject to random testing for alcohol and drugs at any time and at any place while they are on duty. The Safety Board concludes that postaccident test data for fatally injured railroad employees indicate greater alcohol and drug use among maintenance-of-way employees than among railroad employees subject to random and postaccident testing requirements.

Congress has recognized the deterrent effect of random testing in the United States Armed Forces. In passing the Omnibus Transportation Employee Testing Act of 1991, Public Law No. 102-143, Congress specifically noted that

---

[18] R.C. Baselt, *Drug Effects on Psychomotor Performance* (Foster City, CA: Biomedical Publications, 2001).

The testing of uniformed personnel of the Armed Forces has shown that the most effective deterrent to abuse of alcohol and use of illegal drugs is increased testing, especially random testing.

The FRA has also recognized the deterrent effect of random testing in the railroad industry. The FRA has stated[19] the following:

The deterrent effect of random drug testing, which was implemented in 1988-1989, most certainly influenced the dramatic reduction in post-accident positives from 41 in 1988 to only 17 in 1990.

The Safety Board undertook a safety study to review the first full year of implementation of the FRA's alcohol and drug testing rules, which were in effect before the Omnibus Transportation Employee Testing Act of 1991. These rules did not apply to maintenance-of-way employees, maintenance-of-equipment employees, or others in safety-sensitive positions. The study found that limiting the applicability of alcohol and drug testing to only hours-of-service employees restricts the potential effectiveness of the FRA rule to control alcohol and drug use.

As result of the 1988 safety study, the Safety Board made 11 safety recommendations to the FRA. One of those recommendations, which is relevant to the Woburn investigation, asked the FRA to require toxicological testing of all employees in safety-sensitive positions. The FRA subsequently informed the Safety Board (3 years after the 1991 Act) that after reviewing the issue on several occasions, it had decided that employees covered by the Hours of Service Act occupy the most sensitive positions and that expansion of those tested would cause either an excessive burden or an overdelegation of decisional authority to the railroad supervisor in the field. Based on the FRA's response, the Board classified Safety Recommendation R-88-23 "Closed-Reconsidered." However, the Board stated that it would continue to monitor this issue closely.

As this accident and a review of 10 years of data show, a regulation to cover all safety-sensitive employees is overdue. The FRA data from postaccident alcohol and drug testing indicate that maintenance-of-way employees are about three times more likely to have positive test results than are covered employees (19.23 percent vs. 6.56 percent). This difference is attributable to the deterrent value of the FRA's random testing program to which covered employees are subject but maintenance-of-way employees are not. The Safety Board concludes that the FRA's random alcohol and drug testing program has been a deterrent to alcohol and drug use by covered employees, as evidenced by their significantly lower positive rate in postaccident tests than maintenance-of-way employees who are not subject to random testing. The Safety Board recommends that the FRA revise the definition of "covered employee" under 49 CFR Part 219 for purposes of Congressionally mandated alcohol and controlled substances testing programs

---

[19] 66 *Federal Register* 64004.

to encompass all employees and agents performing safety-sensitive functions, as described in 49 CFR 209.301 and 209.303. Further, the Brotherhood of Maintenance of Way Employes Division can promptly take action to help its members address issues they may have with alcohol and drug abuse. Therefore, the Safety Board recommends that the Brotherhood of Maintenance of Way Employes Division promote the prevention of alcohol and drug abuse by assisting its members in addressing awareness, education, and treatment options.

CONCLUSIONS

Findings

1. The signal system performance and the train engineer's performance were not factors in this accident.

2. The train dispatcher forgot about the maintenance-of-way work crew and removed the blocking from the wrong track segment, allowing train 322 to enter the work area on a clear signal indication.

3. The maintenance-of-way work crew did not apply a shunting device; therefore, additional signal protection did not exist for the track segment they occupied, and the dispatcher's screen did not indicate the track segment was occupied.

4. Massachusetts Bay Commuter Railroad maintenance-of-way work crews routinely reduced safety by not using shunting devices when performing jobs that required the track to be out of service.

5. Massachusetts Bay Commuter Railroad's management failed to ensure that maintenance-of-way work crews were using shunting devices as required.

6. Maintenance-of-way work crews on all railroads who depend on the train dispatcher for signal protection need redundant protection to restrict train movements into work areas.

7. The foreman's performance would likely have been measurably impaired at the time of the accident by his recent use of marijuana.

8. Postaccident test data for fatally injured railroad employees indicate greater alcohol and drug use among maintenance-of-way employees than among railroad employees subject to random and postaccident testing requirements.

9. The Federal Railroad Administration's random alcohol and drug testing program has been a deterrent to alcohol and drug use by covered employees, as evidenced by their significantly lower positive rate in postaccident tests than maintenance-of-way employees who are not subject to random testing.

Probable Cause

The National Transportation Safety Board determines that the probable cause of the January 9, 2007, collision of train 322 with a track maintenance vehicle near Woburn, Massachusetts, was the failure of the train dispatcher to maintain blocking that provided signal protection for the track segment occupied by the maintenance-of-way work crew, and the failure of the work crew to apply a shunting device that would have provided redundant signal protection for their track segment. Contributing to the accident was Massachusetts Bay Commuter Railroad's failure to ensure that maintenance-of-way work crews applied shunting devices as required.

RECOMMENDATIONS

As a result of its investigation of the January 9, 2007, collision between southbound Massachusetts Bay Transportation Authority passenger train 322 operated by the Massachusetts Bay Commuter Railroad and a track maintenance vehicle near Woburn, Massachusetts, the National Transportation Safety Board makes the following safety recommendations:

To the Federal Railroad Administration:

> Advise railroads of the need to examine their train dispatching systems and procedures to ensure that appropriate safety redundancies are in place for establishing protection and preventing undesired removal of protection for roadway workers receiving track occupancy authority. (R-08-05)

> Require redundant signal protection, such as shunting, for maintenance-of-way work crews who depend on the train dispatcher to provide signal protection. (R-08-06)

> Revise the definition of "covered employee" under 49 *Code of Federal Regulations* Part 219 for purposes of Congressionally mandated alcohol and controlled substances testing programs to encompass all employees and agents performing safety-sensitive functions, as described in 49 *Code of Federal Regulations* 209.301 and 209.303. (R-08-07)

To the Brotherhood of Maintenance of Way Employes Division:

> Promote the prevention of alcohol and drug abuse by assisting your members in addressing awareness, education, and treatment options. (R-08-08)

BY THE NATIONAL TRANSPORTATION SAFETY BOARD

Mark V. Rosenker
Chairman

Robert L. Sumwalt
Vice Chairman

Deborah A. P. Hersman
Member

Kathryn O'Leary Higgins
Member

Steven R. Chealander
Member

Adopted: March 18, 2008

APPENDIX A

Investigation

The National Transportation Safety Board was notified of the Massachusetts Bay Transportation Authority passenger train 322 collision with the maintenance equipment near Woburn, Massachusetts, about 4:20 p.m., on January 9, 2007. The investigator-in-charge was launched from the Safety Board's Los Angeles Regional Office. No Board Member was on scene.

Parties to the investigation included the Federal Railroad Administration, the Massachusetts Bay Transportation Authority, the Massachusetts Bay Commuter Railroad, the Brotherhood of Locomotive Engineers and Trainmen, the United Transportation Union, and the Brotherhood of Maintenance of Way Employes Division.